LIFE IN THE PAST

ANCIENT EGYPT

Jane Bingham

Adapted from an original text by Clare Hibbert

FRANKLIN WATTS
LONDON•SYDNEY

First published in 2009 by Franklin Watts

Copyright © 2009 Arcturus Publishing Limited

Franklin Watts
338 Euston Road
London NW1 3BH

Franklin Watts Australia
Level 17/207 Kent Street, Sydney, NSW 2000

Produced by Arcturus Publishing Limited,
26/27 Bickels Yard, 151–153 Bermondsey Street, London SE1 3HA

Life in the Past is based on the series *Rich and Poor*, published by Franklin Watts.

Editor: Alex Woolf
Designer: Tim Mayer and Mike Reynolds
Illustrator: Adam Hook
Picture researcher: Glass Onion Pictures

Picture Credits
Art Archive: 4 (Egyptian Museum, Cairo / Dagli Orti), 6 (Egyptian Museum, Cairo / Dagli Orti), 7 (Dagli Orti), 8 (Musée du Louvre, Paris / Dagli Orti), 9 (Ragab Papyrus Institute, Cairo / Dagli Orti), 11 (Musée du Louvre, Paris / Dagli Orti), 12 (Egyptian Museum, Cairo / Dagli Orti [A]), 13 (Egyptian Museum, Turin / Dagli Orti), 14 (Musée du Louvre, Paris / Dagli Orti), 15 (Carthage Museum / Dagli Orti [A]), 18 (Egyptian Museum, Cairo / Dagli Orti [A]), 19 (Musée du Louvre, Paris / Dagli Orti), 20 (British Museum, London / Jacqueline Hyde), 21 (British Museum, London / Dagli Orti [A]), 22 (Egyptian Museum, Cairo / Dagli Orti), 24 (Dagli Orti), 25 (Musée du Louvre, Paris / Dagli Orti), 28 (Pharaonic Village, Cairo / Dagli Orti), 29 (British Museum, London / Jacqueline Hyde).
Bridgeman Art Library: 27 (British Museum, London).
British Museum: 17.
Shutterstock: cover (Holger Mette).

Every attempt has been made to clear copyright. Should there be any inadvertent omission, please apply to the publisher for rectification.

A CIP catalogue record for this book is available from the British Library.

Dewey Decimal Classification Number: 932

ISBN 978 0 7496 9043 4

Printed in China

Franklin Watts is a division of Hachette Children's Books, an Hachette UK Company
www.hachette.co.uk

CONTENTS

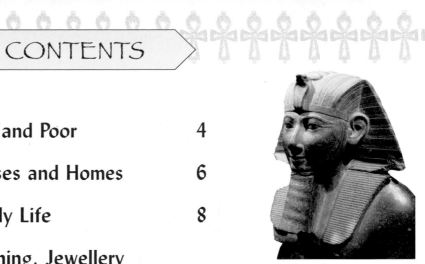

High Life

The richest person in ancient Egypt was the ruler, or pharaoh. People saw the pharaoh as a god. He ruled over the **Two Lands** of Upper and Lower Egypt.

Some people in Egypt earned a lot of money. **Scribes** and doctors were very well paid. Skilled painters and jewellers grew rich too.

Nobles and Priests

After the pharaoh, the next richest group were the nobles. They enjoyed a life of luxury. The chief priests were also very wealthy.

Pharaohs wore a special headdress and a false beard.

Ruler and God

This description of a pharaoh comes from a stone tablet:

'He is Re [the sun god]… the one who **illuminates** the Two Lands more than the sun.'

From the Sehetepibre **Stele** (1900s) BCE

Low Life

Most people in Egypt were poor. They worked hard and lived very simply. Peasants worked long hours in the fields. Builders constructed huge temples from stone. Their work was very tiring and they often died young.

Life was not much better for soldiers and sailors. Servants, dancers and acrobats had hard lives too.

This servant is bringing food. He carries two fans to cool his master.

A Slave's Life

The poorest people in Egypt were the slaves. Some slaves worked as servants for the rich. Some did dangerous jobs in mines.

Mud Mansions

This model shows a house and garden. It was made by ancient Egyptian craftworkers.

The Egyptians lived in houses made from mud. Even the pharaoh's palace was built from mud bricks.

The houses of the rich had brightly painted walls. All their furniture was beautifully carved. Beds often had legs shaped like animals.

Town and Country

The nobles lived in cities, such as Memphis or Thebes. They had tall houses with plenty of rooms. The houses had a shady terrace on the roof.

Many nobles also owned a villa in the country. Their country houses were surrounded by gardens.

Not Much Room

Love your Home!

Some rich people let their houses stand empty. But a priest gave some wise advice:

'He who loves his house so as to dwell in it warms it to its beams.'

From *The Instruction of 'Onchsheshonqy*

Poor people lived in simple mud-brick houses. Inside, there were areas for sleeping, eating and praying. People cooked outside to avoid the risk of fire.

Poor families had very little furniture. They used stools, **headrests** and storage chests. In summer, their houses were very hot, so families often slept on the roof.

Barracks

Builders and soldiers lived in **barracks**. They slept in dormitories and ate together in a dining hall.

This is a ruined town at Deir el Medina. It was home to builders and craftworkers.

For Richer...

Egyptian boys and girls married very young. Usually their parents chose a partner for them.

Very rich couples often married someone in their family. Some pharaohs even married their sisters.

When they got married, the couple signed a contract. They agreed to share all their property.

Pharaoh Akhenaten holds hands with his wife, Nefertiti.

Childcare

Egyptian wives stayed at home. They ran the home and brought up their children.

Wealthy women had many servants to help look after the children.

...For Poorer

This painting shows a noblewoman giving birth. She is helped by midwives.

Like the rich, most poor couples had an arranged marriage. Their parents chose a suitable partner from the same class. But a few couples married for love.

Poor couples did not usually sign a contract. Their marriage began when they set up home together.

How to Treat a Wife

The **scribe** Ani gave some good advice to his son:

'Do not control your wife in her house when you know she is efficient. Do not say to her "Where is it?, Get it!", when she has put it in the right place.'

From *Instructions of Ani*

Giving Birth

Some women had as many as 15 children. Childbirth was a dangerous business. Roughly a third of all babies died. Many mothers died soon after giving birth.

Only the Best

The rich wore clothes made from fine linen. Women had long, flowing dresses. Men wore short, **pleated** kilts. Sometimes men wore a woollen cape.

Clothes were bleached white, but people wore colourful jewellery. Men and women wore wide collars made from rows of beads.

A Prince's Gifts to the Pharaoh

'… armlets, gold bracelets, necklaces, collars inlaid with gemstones … and clothing of royal linen … all the best of my weaving workshop.'

From the Piye Victory **Stele**

Rich women wore gold jewellery set with precious stones.

Hair and Make-Up

Rich men and women rubbed scented oil into the skin. They also wore dramatic eye make-up.

Most people shaved their heads and wore wigs. The wigs were made of plaited human hair.

Coarse Cloth

The poor wore clothes made from coarse cloth. Women wore simple dresses. Men tied a piece of cloth around the waist.

Wives made all the clothes for their family – but the husbands washed the clothes. They had to watch out for crocodiles!

Cheap Jewellery

Even very poor people wore jewellery. They had necklaces and rings made from shells or beaten copper.

Poor men and women rubbed cheap castor oil into the skin. It smelt bad, but it kept the skin soft.

Most poor Egyptians went barefoot. Some servants wore sandals made from reeds.

Fine Feasts

Only the rich could afford to eat meat. They ate a wide range of meat, including beef, goose, goat and duck. Sometimes they even ate ostrich.

Roast meats were served at grand feasts. Many of the dishes were flavoured with spices.

The rich also enjoyed cakes, biscuits and bread. Some bakers made cakes that looked like crocodiles!

Fruit and Wine

In the towns, rich people had small courtyard gardens. They grew fresh vegetables and fruit. They used their grapes to make wine.

A husband and wife share a feast. The table is piled high with food!

Bread and Beer

Everyone in Egypt ate bread. It was sometimes flavoured with herbs or dates.

The poor ate the same vegetables as the rich. These included lettuces, cucumbers, leeks and onions. People also ate melons, figs, dates and pomegranates.

Most poor people did not drink water. Instead they made a kind of beer from barley.

Gifts from the River

Some Egyptians caught fish in the Nile. They also used nets to catch river ducks.

An Egyptian model of a kitchen. In the centre are barrels of beer.

Too Much Wine

This is part of a story about Pharaoh Amasis:

'Pharaoh drank an extremely large quantity of wine…. Morning came, and Pharaoh was unable to raise himself.'

From *The Tale of Amasis and the Skipper*

Costly Care

Part of an Egyptian medical text. It gives instructions for making a medicine.

When the rich were sick, they visited a doctor. Egyptian doctors made medicines from plants and herbs. They could also stitch up wounds and mend broken bones.

There were doctors for different parts of the body, such as the eyes, teeth or stomach. The pharaoh kept many doctors in his palace, ready to treat any problem.

Medical Notes

These notes were written by an Egyptian doctor:

'The patient ... feels thirsty during the night. His saliva has the taste of unripe fruits. His muscles pain him ...'

From the Berlin **Papyrus**

Student Doctors

Only boys from noble families could train as doctors. Medical students studied ancient texts. They also examined dead bodies.

Medicines and Magic

Poor people lived very close together. This meant that diseases could spread very fast. Many people died from **malaria** and **smallpox**.

People also suffered injuries at work. If they fell ill, the poor could not afford a doctor. They had to buy medicine from a chemist. Often they made their own medicines at home.

Magic Charms

Some poor people relied on magic. They wore a lucky charm called an **amulet**. People hoped that the amulet would protect them from disease.

Some amulets were small models. This amulet shows the god Horus. People believed that Horus watched out for evil spirits.

Lessons and Sport

Some wealthy boys trained for a special job. They learned to be a **scribe**, a doctor, a priest or an architect. If a boy wanted to be a scribe, he had to start school at five.

Other wealthy children stayed at home. They learnt all the skills they needed from their parents. Boys also learned swimming, riding and archery.

Private Tutors

Princes and princesses had private tutors at home. The tutors taught them to read, write and do sums.

Young scribes learned to write hieroglyphs. These were a kind of picture writing.

Advice to a Young Scribe

'O scribe, do not be idle…. Write with your hand, recite with your mouth, and converse with those more knowledgeable than you.'

From the **Papyrus** Anastasi

Working Children

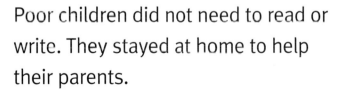

These are simple spinning tops.
Children could spin a top by hand
or wind a string round it and pull.

Poor children did not need to read or write. They stayed at home to help their parents.

Most children learned to do their parents' jobs. Peasants' children worked in the fields. Servants' children helped to prepare food.

Builders' sons joined a building gang. They learned how to cut and carve stone.

Fun and Games

Poor children started work when were five. Before that, they had fun. Children played with simple toys such as dolls, balls and tops.

Top Jobs

Everybody worked in ancient Egypt. Even the pharaoh kept very busy. He ruled the country and controlled the army.

There were plenty of good jobs for noblemen. Some nobles worked as high priests, architects or **scribes**. Others collected taxes or judged criminals.

Scribes recorded trials in the law courts. They also kept records for the landowners.

A few noblewomen had top jobs, too. There were some female scribes and at least one woman judge.

Skilled Work

Skilled craftworkers earned a lot of money. Some of them designed stunning jewellery. Others painted **murals,** made fine pottery or carved elegant furniture.

Tough Toil

This painting shows peasants working hard in the fields.

Most poor people worked incredibly hard. They also had to do national service. This was important work for the pharaoh, such as repairing a dam.

When there was a problem, the pharaoh called on everyone to help. But rich people paid money instead. So the poor did all the work.

Hard Labour

Many poor people worked on the land. They hardly earned enough to feed their families. Soldiers also had a very tough job.

A Soldier's Life

'His **rations** and his water are upon his shoulder like the load of an ass.... The **vertebrae** of his back are broken.... He stops work [only] to keep watch.'

From the **Papyrus** Anastasi

Fun for the Rich

Wealthy Egyptians loved holding parties. Party guests enjoyed delicious food and drink. They also watched dancing girls and listened to musicians playing flutes, harps and cymbals.

Favourite Pastimes

In their spare time, Egyptian noblemen liked to go hunting with dogs. They often hunted for birds in the river marshes.

Board games were very popular, and the game of *senet* was a favourite.

Senet was a game for two players. Each player moved their pieces round the board.

Hunting by the Nile

A nobleman described the joys of hunting:

'A happy day when we go down to the marsh … [to] snare birds and catch many fishes…. We shall trap birds and shall light a brazier to Sobek [the crocodile god].'

From *The Pleasures of Fishing and Fowling*

Songs and Stories

Poor people often told stories to each other. Some stories told the adventures of heroes. Others were myths about the gods.

Music and Dance

Sometimes people played music while they worked. They used rhythm sticks and drums to beat out a simple tune. People also played music for relaxation. Love songs were especially popular.

Some people earned their living by music and dance. Dancers and musicians entertained the rich at their parties. They also performed at funerals.

This wall painting shows dancers and musicians at a feast.

Travelling in Style

On land, most nobles travelled in a litter. This was a chair on poles that was carried by servants. Some very rich men rode in chariots.

Boats on the Nile

Most people in Egypt lived beside the River Nile, so they usually travelled by boat. The rich had their own private boats, made from cedarwood.

Boats sailed south down the river, blown by the wind. When boats travelled north, a team of oarsmen had to row hard.

This painting shows Pharaoh Tutankhamun in his chariot. He is riding into battle.

Boats and Beasts

Even the poor travelled by boat. They made simple rafts from reeds.

Larger boats carried passengers and cargo. Barges carried blocks of stone to be used for building.

Teams of builders moved the stone from the riverbank to the building sites. It is likely that they used strong ropes and dragged the blocks across the sand.

Land Travel

When they were on land, poor people walked. Cattle and donkeys carried heavy loads.

A Traveller's Song

'I am sailing downstream on the ferry,

[Guided] by the hand of the helmsman,

With my bundle of reeds on my shoulder.

I am bound for [Memphis].'

From the Love Songs of **Papyrus** Harris 500

Fishermen speared fish from small reed boats. They were in great danger from crocodiles!

Sacred Ceremonies

The people of Egypt worshipped many gods. Two of their main gods were Re the sun god and Isis the goddess of love. People also saw their pharaoh as a god. The pharaoh had many religious duties.

A Pharaoh's Duties

'Perform the monthly priestly service, don white sandals …

Enter into the holy place, eat bread in the house of the god'

From the Teaching for King Merykara (c. 2025–1700 BCE)

Houses of the Gods

Priests and priestesses lived in the temples of the gods. They chanted prayers, played sacred music and performed dances.

Priests also gave offerings to the gods. Ordinary people were not allowed in the temples.

The Temple of Amun at Karnak was one of Egypt's most holy places.

Festivals and Shrines

Everyone in Egypt took part in the religious festivals. Crowds gathered to watch as priests carried statues of the gods.

People also visited small shrines. There they prayed to the gods and gave offerings.

Sometimes people paid for a stone tablet called a stele. The words of their prayer were carved on the **stele**.

Household Gods

Most families had a shrine in their house. This was a small alcove where they kept a statue of a god. Many homes had a shrine to Taweret.

Taweret was the goddess of childbirth. She took the form of a hippopotamus.

Making Mummies

All the ancient Egyptians believed in the afterlife. They thought they would need their bodies after they died.

Rich people had their bodies preserved as mummies. This process was performed by **embalmers**.

First the embalmers removed all the insides, except for the heart. Then they filled the body with a kind of salt. This dried everything out.

Wrapping Up

After 40 days, the body was filled with linen or sawdust. Then the embalmers wrapped it in bandages.

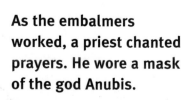

As the embalmers worked, a priest chanted prayers. He wore a mask of the god Anubis.

Common Graves

Poor people could not afford to be embalmed. But they were buried with a few belongings. People believed they would use these things in the next life.

This man lived in Egypt around 5,200 years ago. The dry desert sand preserved his body.

Fuss-Free Funerals

After they died, most poor people were placed in a simple coffin. Coffins were often made from reeds.

The very poorest people did not have a coffin. Their bodies were thrown into a pit in the desert.

How to Make a Mummy

'First with the crooked iron tool they draw out the brain through the nostrils ... [next] they make a cut along the side and take out the whole contents of the belly ...'

From Herodotus's *Histories*

Treasure-Filled Tombs

After a body was mummified, it was placed in a coffin. Then the coffin was put in a tomb.

Inside the tomb were the dead person's jewels, weapons and furniture. Paintings on the walls showed their house and family.

People hoped the afterlife would be just the same as their life on earth.

Tomb Types

The most impressive tombs are the pyramids. They were built for the early pharaohs. Later pharaohs were buried in tombs under the ground.

This is one of the rooms inside the tomb of Pharaoh Tutankhamun.

Heavenly Hopes

Poor people were buried with a few belongings and some food. Like the rich, they believed they would travel to the afterlife.

Journey to the Afterlife

The journey to the afterlife was very hard. There were evil gods, snakes and crocodiles to fight.

How to Enter the Afterlife

Only the pure could enter the afterlife:

'A man should [be] pure and clean … shod in white sandals, painted with black eye-paint, **anointed** with the finest **myrrh** oil …' From the Book of the Dead

Finally, a person's heart was weighed. If his heart was heavy with lies, he was eaten by a monster. If his heart was light, he was allowed into the afterlife.

The god Anubis leads a dead person to the afterlife.

All dates are BCE

c. 7000	The first farming villages are built on the banks of the River Nile.
c. 3050	The Two Lands of Upper Egypt and Lower Egypt are united.
c. 3000	The Egyptians start to use hieroglyphs (picture writing).
c. 2650s	The first pyramids are built.
c. 2575–c. 2465	The pyramids and Sphinx are built at Giza (near modern Cairo).
c. 1450	The Egyptian lands are at their largest.
c. 1510	The Egyptians build the Temple of Amun at Karnak.
c. 1500	The world's oldest-known medical text, the Ebers papyrus, is written.
1330s	The boy pharaoh, Tutankhamun, rules Egypt.
524–404	Persian kings rule over Egypt.
332	Alexander the Great invades Egypt with a Greek army. The Greeks start to control Egypt.
51–30	The female pharaoh, Cleopatra, rules Egypt
30	The Romans conquer and start to rule Egypt.

Books

Kingfisher Knowledge: Mummies by John Malam (Kingfisher, 2003)
Men, Women and Children in Ancient Egypt by Jane Bingham (Wayland, 2007)
The Story of the Nile by Anne Millard and illustrated by Steve Noon (Dorling Kindersley, 2003)
Virtual History Tours: Look Around an Egyptian Tomb by Liz Gogerly (Franklin Watts, 2007)

CD-Roms, Videos, DVDs and Audiocassettes

Egypt – Secrets of the Pharaohs (National Geographic, 2002). Video and DVD.
Egyptian Gods and Pharaohs (BBC Audio Books, 2003). CD-Rom and audiocassette.

Websites

www.bbc.co.uk/history/ancient/egyptians/index.shtml
www.ancientegypt.co.uk/menu.html
www.ancient-egypt.org/

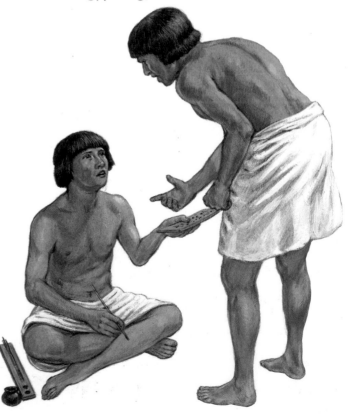

amulet A magic charm.

anointed Rubbed with oil.

barracks Large buildings where soldiers live.

beam A piece of wood that helps to hold up a building.

brazier A small fire in a container.

converse Talk with someone.

don Put on.

embalmer Someone who treats dead bodies so that they do not rot away.

headrest A support for the head. The ancient Egyptians used wooden headrests to support their heads while they slept.

helmsman A person who steers a boat.

hieroglyph A small picture or symbol. The Egyptians wrote using hieroglyphs. Each hieroglyph might stand for a sound or a whole word.

illuminate Light up.

malaria A serious disease that is carried by mosquitoes in hot countries. In ancient Egyptian times, people often died from malaria.

mural A wall painting.

myrrh oil A strong-smelling oil that is very precious and expensive. Myrrh oil comes from a tree known as the incense tree.

papyrus A reed that grows by the River Nile. The ancient Egyptians used papyrus to make paper. The word *papyrus* also means a scroll.

pleated Having many folds of cloth.

rations Supplies of food.

recite Repeat something from memory. Some ancient Egyptian children learned to recite poetry.

scribe In ancient Egypt, a scribe was someone who wrote things down.

smallpox A serious disease that was spread through the air. In ancient Egyptian times, people often died from smallpox. They had a very high temperature and itchy, red spots.

snare Trap.

stele A piece of stone with writing on it.

Two Lands The two countries that made up ancient Egypt. The two lands were Upper Egypt and Lower Egypt. They were united into a single kingdom around 2900 BCE.

vertebrae Sections of backbone.

Page numbers in **bold** refer to illustrations.